# Polar Bear

## Shrinking Ice

by Stephen Person

Consultant: BJ Kirschhoffer
Director of Field Operations
Polar Bears International
www.polarbearsinternational.org

BEARPORT
PUBLISHING

New York, New York

## Credits

Cover and Title Page, © Peter Kirillov/Shutterstock; TOC, © Witold Kaszkin/Shutterstock; 4, © Mitsuaki Iwago/Minden Pictures; 5, © Thomas Sbampato/Alaska Stock LLC/Alamy; 6, © BJ Kirschhoffer; 8, © Chris Wallace/Alamy; 9, © Barbara Trombley/Accent Alaska; 10L, © Steve Bloom Images/Alamy; 10R, © Science Faction/SuperStock; 11, © age fotostock /SuperStock; 12T, © Steven Kazlowski/NPL/Minden Pictures; 12B, © Daniel J. Cox/NaturalExposures; 13, © Staffan Widstrand/ Staffan Widstrand Photography; 14, © Science Faction/SuperStock; 15T, © Flip Nicklin/Minden Pictures/Getty Images; 16, © Rinie Van Meurs/Foto Natura/Minden Pictures; 17T, Courtesy of USGS; 17B, © Daniel J. Cox/NaturalExposures; 18T, © All Canada Photos/SuperStock; 18B, © Robert Harding Picture Library/SuperStock; 19, © M. Cohen/SuperStock; 20, © Chris Schenk/Foto Natura/ Minden Pictures; 21, © Paul J. Richards/AFP/Getty Images; 23L, © lexaarts/Shutterstock; 23R, © ssuaphotos/Shutterstock; 24L, © Olivier Grunewald/OSF/Photolibrary; 24R, © Michael S. Nolan/ SeaPics; 25, © 2d Alan King/Alamy; 26, © Tohoku Color Agency/Japan Images/Getty Images; 27, © Paul Nicklen/National Geographic/Getty Images; 28, © Bruce & Jan Lichtenberger/SuperStock; 29T, © Steven J. Kazlowski/Alamy; 29B, © age fotostock/SuperStock; 31, © Witold Kaszkin/ Shutterstock; 32, © Ecostock/Shutterstock.

Publisher: Kenn Goin
Editorial Director: Adam Siegel
Creative Director: Spencer Brinker
Photo Researcher: James O'Connor

*Library of Congress Cataloging-in-Publication Data*

Person, Stephen.
  Polar bear : shrinking ice / by Stephen Person.
      p. cm. — (Built for cold—arctic animals)
  Includes bibliographical references and index.
  ISBN-13: 978-1-61772-129-8 (library binding)
  ISBN-10: 1-61772-129-8 (library binding)
 1. Polar bear—Juvenile literature. I. Title.
  QL737.C27P422 2011
  599.786—dc22

                           2010038750

For more information, write to Bearport Publishing Company, Inc., 101 Fifth Avenue, Suite 6R, New York, New York 10003. Printed in the United States of America in North Mankato, Minnesota.

113010
10810CGA

10 9 8 7 6 5 4 3 2 1

# Contents

# The Polar Bear Capital

It was early September 2009. **Researcher** BJ Kirschhoffer (KURSH-*hoff*-ur) was in Churchill, Canada, to study polar bears. He'd come to the right place. So many bears live near Churchill that it's known as the polar bear capital of the world!

More than 1,000 polar bears spend part of the year near the town of Churchill.

BJ looked out the window of his **Tundra** Buggy, a huge truck built to travel over snow and ice. "There were bears all over the place," BJ reported, "but some did not look healthy." Many of them were skinny. BJ could even see their ribs through their white fur. "I knew that something was very wrong," he said. These were not well-fed bears.

**People come from all over the world to see the bears of Churchill.**

the Tundra Buggy

The world polar bear **population** is 20,000 to 25,000. About 60 percent of the bears live in Canada.

# A Freezing Home

To find out more about the skinny bears, BJ turned to Ian Stirling and Andrew Derocher, **biologists** who have been studying the animals for more than 30 years. Ian and Andrew had also noticed changes in the polar bears' weight. Their research on polar bears and their **habitat** helped explain why the animals weren't finding enough food.

BJ studies polar bears in both Canada and northern Alaska. Here, he is lying in the snow near the entrance to the home of a mother polar bear and her cubs.

When scientists such as Ian and Andrew study polar bears, they work in the **Arctic region**—the only part of the world where polar bears live. It is also one of the coldest places on Earth. Winter temperatures average −29°F (−34°C), and northern parts of the Arctic get much colder. To stay warm, the scientists have to put on layer after layer of clothing. Still, they can only stay outside for a few hours. Polar bears, however, are amazing. This freezing world is their home. How do polar bears survive in this kind of **climate**?

# Polar Bears in the Wild

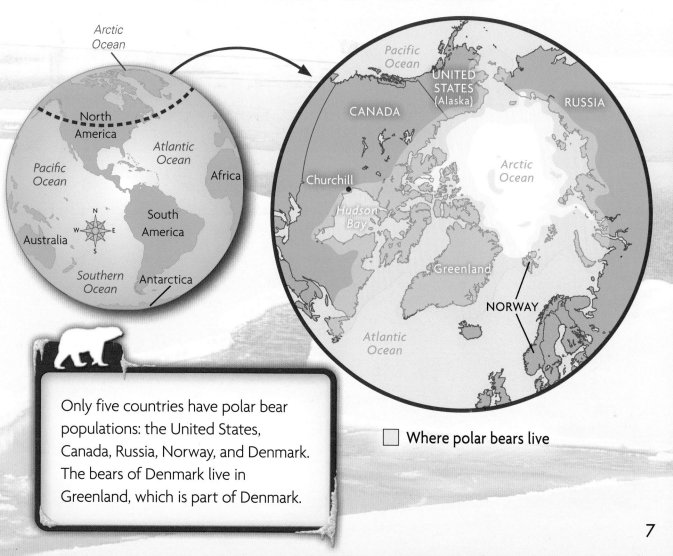

Only five countries have polar bear populations: the United States, Canada, Russia, Norway, and Denmark. The bears of Denmark live in Greenland, which is part of Denmark.

☐ Where polar bears live

# Staying Warm

Polar bears can live in the Arctic because they are **adapted** to life in the cold. The bears' bodies are covered with thick fur. Beneath their skin is a layer of fat called blubber, which can be up to 4.5 inches (11.4 cm) thick. Both fur and blubber act as **insulation**, keeping the cold out and the bears' body heat in.

Polar bears are very careful to clean their fur after meals. When fur is dirty or matted together, it does not trap a bear's body heat as well.

Even with thick fur and blubber, however, bears can get cold in the winter. To protect themselves from icy winds, they sometimes dig holes in the snow. During long **blizzards**, bears can stay in these holes for days, allowing the falling snow to cover their bodies.

Snow is cold, but it's also good insulation. Just like a blanket, a layer of snow helps keep heat from leaving a bear's body.

# Staying Cool

Polar bears are so well adapted to life in the Arctic that they are more likely to get hot than cold. This explains why polar bears usually walk very slowly and rest often. When bears move quickly, their bodies create heat. The bears' blubber and fur keep this heat inside their bodies. As a result, bears can easily **overheat**, even in the Arctic. When bears get hot, they roll in the snow or dive into the ocean to cool off.

**These bears are rolling in the snow to cool off.**

**Polar bears can run as fast as 25 miles per hour (40 kph). They can run only for short distances, however, because their bodies quickly get too hot.**

Luckily, the bodies of polar bears are also adapted for swimming. The bears' thick layer of blubber helps them float in the water. They also have huge paws, up to 12 inches (30 cm) across. Bears use these big paws to paddle and steer as they swim.

Bears swim in the icy Arctic water to cool off. They also swim to clean themselves after eating. They can stay underwater for up to two minutes.

Scientists have seen bears swim up to 60 miles (97 km) without stopping. They can swim more than 6 miles per hour (10 kph)—that's faster than Olympic champion swimmers such as Michael Phelps.

# At Home on the Ice

Polar bears spend most of their lives at sea. In fact, the animal's scientific name—*Ursus maritimus*—means "sea bear." Polar bears don't live in the water, however. They live *on* the water—that is, on frozen sections of the ocean known as sea ice.

The thick black pads on the bottoms of a polar bear's paws are covered with small bumps. The bumps help the bear walk on sea ice without slipping.

In the Arctic, large flat pieces of sea ice form each year when temperatures drop in the fall. The bears live on the ice until it melts the following spring. On sea ice, polar bears are experts at catching their favorite **prey**—the ringed seal.

Polar bears are not well adapted for hunting in water or on land. They are good swimmers but not quick enough to catch seals in the water. On land, they quickly overheat when they run.

**Polar bears jump or swim to get from one piece of ice to another.**

# Seal-Killing Machines

According to biologist Tom Smith, a scientist who studies Arctic animals, polar bears are highly skilled "seal-killing machines." Most of the polar bear's diet is made up of ringed seals. Catching these animals, however, takes a lot of skill—and patience.

Polar bears, such as this one, sometimes eat whales that get stuck in sea ice or stranded on land.

Like all **mammals**, seals breathe air. They make small holes in the sea ice, called **aglus**, so that they can stick their heads out of the water to breathe. Polar bears know this, and once they find an aglu, they will wait beside it for hours—sometimes for days. When a seal comes up to breathe, look out! The bear snaps its jaws around the seal's head, flips it onto the ice, and begins to eat it.

**Ringed seals are quick, smart, and hard to catch. This seal checks for bears as it comes to the surface. Ringed seals can stay underwater for up to 45 minutes.**

Most polar bear hunts are not successful. A polar bear may catch one seal about every four or five days. After catching a seal, polar bears will eat as much as 100 pounds (45 kg) in a single meal.

# Into the Den

Polar bears don't use sea ice just for hunting. It is also important for **reproduction**. Polar bears **mate** on the ice, usually in April or May. After mating, female bears must load up on seal meat and blubber. Pregnant bears have to gain more than 400 pounds (181 kg) to survive the huge challenges ahead.

**A polar bear eating a seal it has caught**

In October or early November, a pregnant bear will dig a **den**. This tunnel in the deep snow is barely big enough for the bear to fit inside. After entering the den, the mother will not leave it or eat again until spring. She will live on the fat stored in her body. Mothers usually give birth in November or December. The tiny cubs stay in the warm den all winter, feeding on their mother's rich milk.

A scientist looking into a polar bear den

The thick layer of snow around a den helps keep the bears warm inside.

Polar bears most often give birth to two cubs. A **litter** of one or three is also fairly common. A female bear can have about five litters in her lifetime.

# Learning from Mom

Newborn polar bears are only 12 to 14 inches (30 to 36 cm) long and weigh only about one pound (.45 kg)—much smaller than human babies. They grow quickly, however. In March or April, the mother bear breaks out of her snow den and leads her cubs outside. By this time, the cubs weigh about 20 to 30 pounds (9 to 14 kg).

**A three-month-old cub inside its den**

**A mother and her cub coming out of their den**

The bear cubs follow their mother onto the sea ice. After her long winter **fast**, the mother badly needs to catch seals for food. The cubs watch their mother hunt, and share in the meal of fresh meat. Cubs will stay with their mother for about two and a half years, learning how to hunt seals and survive in the Arctic. After that time, they are ready to live on their own.

Mother polar bears are very protective of their young. They will risk their own lives to protect their cubs from animals such as arctic wolves.

Polar bear cubs begin trying to hunt before their first birthday. Most do not succeed in catching a seal until they are more than one year old.

# Climate Clues

Just like their parents, young polar bears spend most of their life on sea ice. BJ thought about this as he watched more and more skinny bears gather in Churchill, Canada, by the shores of Hudson Bay. He knew from Ian and Andrew's research that the bears were waiting for ice to form there. Stuck on the tundra, they would find very little to eat. Why?

These young bears are not really fighting. They are playing. This kind of play is a way for bears to stay strong while they are waiting for sea ice to form.

Polar bears rely on seals for food, and they rely on sea ice to get to the seals. If the ice begins to disappear, then the bears will be in big trouble. They won't be able to reach their food. In fact, that is exactly what is now happening in the Arctic.

Bears near Churchill, such as this one, have to wait until late November for Hudson Bay to freeze. Twenty years ago, the ice formed in early November.

Polar bears usually walk and swim a few hundred miles (km) each year in search of food. Some, however, have traveled as much as 3,000 miles (4,828 km).

# A Warming Planet

Scientists who study Earth's climate report that the Arctic is slowly getting warmer. In recent years, temperatures in the Arctic have been higher than they have been at any other time in the past 400 years. The Arctic is about 1.8 degrees Fahrenheit (1 degree Celsius) warmer than it was just 20 years ago. As a result, the Arctic's sea ice is shrinking.

## Shrinking Sea Ice

Sea ice

Seawater freezes at 28.8°F (−1.8°C). A warmer Arctic means that less water becomes cold enough to freeze. This map shows how much the sea ice in the Arctic shrank between 1982 and 2008.

The warming Arctic is part of a larger problem known as **global warming**. Most scientists agree that human activities are the cause of global warming. When people burn **fossil fuels** to power cars or make electricity, **greenhouse gases** such as **carbon dioxide** are released. These gases trap the sun's heat in Earth's **atmosphere**. The buildup of more and more carbon dioxide and other greenhouse gases is causing Earth's climate to get warmer.

**Power plants and car and truck engines produce most of the carbon dioxide emissions in many parts of the world.**

Some scientists believe that if global warming continues at its current rate, global temperatures are likely to rise by 3 to 7 degrees Fahrenheit (1.7 to 3.9 degrees Celsius) by 2100. They predict that temperatures in the Arctic will rise even faster.

# Mystery Solved

Climate change was the key to solving the skinny bear mystery. Ian and Andrew's research showed that as global temperatures rise, Hudson Bay is freezing a little later each fall. Each spring, the ice is breaking up and melting a little earlier. This means that the polar bears can't spend as much time on the sea ice—or as much time hunting. In 2009, the bears of Hudson Bay had about three weeks less hunting time than they had in 1990.

**When bears can't get onto the sea ice to hunt, they are more likely to search for food near garbage dumps and people's homes. This can be dangerous for both people and bears.**

If global warming continues at its current rate, some scientists predict that Hudson Bay will not freeze at all by 2080.

Because of shrinking sea ice, many bears simply are not getting enough to eat. Studies have shown that the bears of Hudson Bay are smaller than they were 20 years ago. Also, fewer young bears are surviving into adulthood. Hudson Bay's bear population has decreased more than 20 percent since the 1980s.

**Up until about 40 years ago, the main threat to polar bears came from hunters. In 1973, all five nations with polar bear populations agreed to stop most polar bear hunting.**

# Bears on Thin Ice

As the planet continues to warm, polar bears all over the Arctic will face the same challenges as the bears of Hudson Bay. Scientists recently found the bodies of four polar bears that had drowned in the Beaufort Sea, off the **coast** of Alaska. It is unusual for bears to drown, since they are such strong swimmers. The scientists believe that the bears were trying to reach sea ice that was 160 miles (257 km) north of the coast. That's too far to swim, even for polar bears.

As Arctic sea ice shrinks, bears are being forced to swim farther to reach it. Scientists believe that this is causing some bears to drown.

The polar bear is perfectly adapted for life in the harsh Arctic environment. Can it adapt to a warmer Arctic? No one knows for sure. "The good news is there are things we can do to help," said BJ. "By using a bit less fossil fuel, we can release less greenhouse gases. That can help keep the Arctic icy—just how polar bears like it!"

**Some United States government scientists predict that if global warming continues at its current rate, there will be no polar bears left in Alaska by 2050.**

In 2008, the United States listed the polar bear as a **threatened** species under the Endangered Species Act. This law helps protect species that are threatened with **extinction**. Other countries with polar bears have taken similar actions.

# Polar Bear Facts

With warm fur and thick blubber, the polar bear is perfectly adapted for life in the Arctic. Here are some other facts about these amazing animals.

| | |
|---|---|
| **Weight** | male adults weigh from 775 pounds to more than 1,500 pounds (352 to 680 kg); female adults weigh from 330 to 550 pounds (150 to 249 kg) |
| **Height** | males are 8 to 10 feet (2.4 to 3 m) tall when standing on their back legs; females are 6 to 8 feet (1.8 to 2.4 m) tall |
| **Food** | mainly seals, also whales, reindeer, walruses, birds, and eggs |
| **Life Span** | an average of 15 to 18 years in the wild; 30 years or more in zoos; in a Canadian zoo, a polar bear named Debby lived to be 42 years old |
| **Habitat** | Arctic region |
| **Population** | 20,000 to 25,000 |

# More Arctic Animals

The Arctic region is one of the harshest habitats on Earth. Only animals that are adapted to **extreme** cold, such as the polar bear, can survive there. Here are two others.

## Ringed Seal

- The ringed seal is the most common seal in the Arctic region.
- The seals grow up to 5 feet (1.5 m) long and weigh about 150 pounds (68 kg).
- A thick layer of blubber under the seals' skin keeps their bodies warm in icy water and on sea ice.
- The seals' main foods are fish and **crustaceans**, such as shrimp.
- Polar bears are the seals' main **predator**. They also have to look out for walruses and killer whales.

## Arctic Fox

- The arctic fox lives farther north than any other land mammal and can survive temperatures as low as −58°F (−50°C).
- The foxes have the warmest fur of all animals—including polar bears.
- They weigh between 6 and 17 pounds (2.7 and 7.7 kg) and are about 41 inches (104 cm) long.
- During the summer, arctic foxes live on land and feed on small prey such as birds and mouse-like mammals called lemmings.
- In the winter, they often move onto the sea ice. Foxes follow polar bears, hoping a bear will kill a seal and leave some meat behind.

# Glossary

**adapted** (uh-DAP-tid) changed over time to survive in an environment

**aglus** (AG-looz) breathing holes in sea ice that are made by seals

**Arctic region** (ARK-tik REE-juhn) the northernmost area on Earth; it includes the Arctic Ocean, the North Pole, and northern parts of Europe, Asia, and North America, and is one of the coldest areas in the world

**atmosphere** (AT-muhss-fihr) the mixture of gases surrounding Earth

**biologists** (bye-OL-uh-jists) scientists who study plants or animals

**blizzards** (BLIZ-urdz) strong winds combined with snow that make it difficult to see far

**carbon dioxide** (KAR-buhn dye-OK-side) a greenhouse gas that is released when fossil fuels are burned

**climate** (KLYE-mit) patterns of weather over a long period of time

**coast** (KOHST) land that runs along an ocean

**crustaceans** (kruhs-TAY-shuhnz) a group of animals, including crabs, lobsters, and shrimp, that have a hard shell and no backbone and live mostly in the water

**den** (DEN) the home of a wild animal

**extinction** (ek-STINGK-shun) when a type of animal or plant dies out

**extreme** (ek-STREEM) very great or severe

**fast** (FAST) a period of time when an animal does not eat

**fossil fuels** (FOSS-uhl FYOO-uhlz) energy sources made from the remains of plants and animals that died millions of years ago, such as coal, oil, and gas

**global warming** (GLOHB-uhl WORM-ing) the gradual warming of Earth's air and oceans caused by a buildup of greenhouse gases, which trap heat from the sun in Earth's atmosphere

**greenhouse gases** (GREEN-houss GAS-iz) carbon dioxide, methane, and other gases that trap warm air in the atmosphere; the gases responsible for global warming

**habitat** (HAB-uh-tat) the place in the wild where an animal or a plant normally lives

**insulation** (in-suh-LAY-shuhn) something that prevents heat from escaping

**litter** (LIT-ur) a group of baby animals that are born to the same mother at the same time

**mammals** (MAM-uhlz) animals that are warm-blooded, nurse their young with milk, and have hair or fur on their skin

**mate** (MAYT) to come together to produce young

**overheat** (oh-vur-HEET) to become too hot

**population** (pop-yuh-LAY-shuhn) the total number of a kind of animal living in a place

**predator** (PRED-uh-tur) an animal that hunts other animals for food

**prey** (PRAY) animals that are hunted and eaten by other animals

**reproduction** (ree-pruh-DUHK-shuhn) the act of producing babies

**researcher** (REE-sur-chur) a person who studies things or collects information

**threatened** (THRET-uhnd) being in danger

**tundra** (TUHN-druh) cold, treeless land where the ground is always frozen just below the surface

# Bibliography

**Polar Bears International** ("Bear Essentials, Polar Style")
(www.polarbearsinternational.org/polar-bears/bear-essentials-polar-style)

**Sea World** ("Polar Bears")
(www.seaworld.org/animal-info/info-books/polar-bear/)

**U.S. Fish & Wildlife Service** ("About Polar Bears")
(http://alaska.fws.gov/fisheries/mmm/polarbear/pbmain.htm)

# Read More

**Hatkoff, Juliana, Isabella, and Craig, and Dr. Gerald R. Uhlich.** *Knut: How One Little Polar Bear Captivated the World.* New York: Scholastic Press (2007).

**Markle, Sandra.** *Polar Bears (Animal Predators).* Minneapolis, MN: Carolrhoda Books (2004).

**Orme, Helen.** *Polar Bears in Danger (Wildlife Survival).* New York: Bearport (2007).

**Rosing, Norbert, and Elizabeth Carney.** *Face to Face with Polar Bears (Face to Face with Animals).* Washington, D.C.: National Geographic Children's Books (2009).

# Learn More Online

To learn more about polar bears, visit
**www.bearportpublishing.com/BuiltforCold**

# Index

# About the Author

Stephen Person has written many children's books about history, science, and the environment. He lives with his family in Saratoga Springs, New York.